HAPPY BIRTHDAY

TO

....

WITH LOVE FROM

....

And Frank

HAPPY BIRTHDAY—LOVE . . .
Complete Series

Jane Austen

Joan Crawford

Bette Davis

Liam Gallagher

Audrey Hepburn

John Lennon

Bob Marley

Marilyn Monroe

Michelle Obama

Jackie Kennedy Onassis

Elvis Presley

Keith Richards

Frank Sinatra

Elizabeth Taylor

Oscar Wilde

HAPPY BIRTHDAY
Love, Frank

ON YOUR SPECIAL DAY

ENJOY THE WIT AND WISDOM OF

FRANK SINATRA

THE CHAIRMAN OF THE BOARD

Edited by Jade Riley

CELEBRATION BOOKS

THIS IS A CELEBRATION BOOK

Published by Celebration Books 2023
Celebration Books is an imprint of Dean Street Press

Text & Design Copyright © 2023 Celebration Books

All Rights Reserved. No part of this publication may be reproduced, stored in or transmitted in any form or by any means without the written permission of the copyright owner and the publisher of this book.

Cover by DSP

ISBN 978 1 915393 76 0

www.deanstreetpress.co.uk

HAPPY BIRTHDAY—LOVE, FRANK

FRANK Sinatra may have been born to humble immigrant Italian parents in Hoboken, New Jersey, with no musical training, but his way with a song would elevate him to the icon of the 20th century. If he'd been, as he would often croon, a puppet, a pauper, a pirate, a poet, a pawn, and a king, he also was the Chairman of the Board, Old Blue Eyes, the Sultan of Swoon and even Lady Macbeth! In addition, Frank was an actor, a dancer, a civil rights activist, a father and a husband to four different wives. His long list of awards and honors include the Academy Award for *From Here To Eternity*, Golden

Globes, Emmys and Grammy after Grammy. With a repertoire of close to 1,350 songs, 59 studio albums, and 297 singles, Frank's innate ability and love for singing cannot be matched. That he insisted on helping Ella Fitzgerald, Sammy Davis Jr., Nat King Cole and others to succeed in a divided world means he gave us even more that his own music. Beyond entertaining, he raised millions for Israel, stumped for Roosevelt and Kennedy, turned Las Vegas into his personal playground and landed the Presidential Medal of Freedom.

Frank and his Rat Pack of friends were truly the center of the party. Whether drinking at Chasens in Los Angeles, or hitting the golf course in Palm

Springs, Sinatra lived like the King of the World. His Birthday, December 12, has been named Frank Sinatra Day. Italian restaurants all over New York, New Jersey and beyond hold Frank Sinatra parties. And the Empire State Building is lit up in blue. What is it about Frank? Even his first wife remained his loyal friend and confidante until the day he died. There will never be another character so original, so full of spirit, feistiness and love. Oh, Frank, You make us feel so young!

Frank Sinatra

"Let's start the action!"

"You've got to be on the ball from the minute you step out into that spotlight.

> The best revenge is massive success.

> A simple 'I love you' means more than money.

A man doesn't know what happiness is until he's married. By then it's too late.

Alcohol may be man's worst enemy, but the bible says love your enemy.

A well-balanced girl is the one who has an empty head and a full sweater.

I like intelligent women. When you go out, it shouldn't be a staring contest.

"I've been thinking about why you have to be famous to get an award for helping other people.

"Fear is the enemy of logic.

"

> I believe in you and me. I believe in nature, in the birds, the sea, the sky, in everything I can see or that there is real evidence for. If these things are what you mean by God, then I believe in God.

"Don't hide your scars—they make you who you are.

I am a thing of beauty.

"Cock your hat—angles are attitudes.

> Dean Martin is an absolute, unqualified drunk. And if we ever develop an Olympic drinking team, he's gonna be the coach.

Dare to wear the foolish clown face.

Basically, I'm for anything that gets you through the night—be it prayer, tranquilizers or a bottle of Jack Daniels.

"You lie awake and think about the girl. You never, ever think of counting sheep."

Don't respond to negativity with more negativity. Just put your head down and prove your critics wrong.

Fresh air makes me throw up. I can't handle it. I'd rather be around three Denobili cigars blowing in my face all night.

I believe that God knows what each of us wants and needs. It's not necessary for us to make it to church on Sunday to reach Him. You can find Him anyplace.

> If you don't know the guy on the other side of the world, love him anyway because he's just like you. He has the same dreams, the same hopes and fears. It's one world, pal. We're all neighbors.

My friendships were formed out of affection, mutual respect, and a feeling of having something strong in common. These are eternal values that cannot be racially classified. This is the way I look at race.

If you possess something but you can't give it away, then you don't possess it . . . it possesses you.

"Hell hath no fury like a hustler with a literary agent.

I'm just a singer, Elvis was the embodiment of the whole American culture.

I feel sorry for people who don't drink, because when they wake up in the morning, that is the best they are going to feel all day.

You treat a lady like a dame, and a dame like a lady.

If power doesn't mean that you have the opportunity to work with the people that you love, then you haven't really got any.

"Critics don't bother me because if I do badly, I know I'm bad before they even write it. And if I'm good, I know I'm good. I know best about myself, so a critic doesn't anger me.

Religion is a deeply personal thing in which man and God go it alone together, without the witch doctor in the middle.

"Love is when you want to sing every day and night. Without fee and a manager.

I'm supposed to have a PhD on the subject of women. But the truth is I've flunked more often than not. I'm very fond of women; I admire them. But, like all men, I don't understand them.

"I'm for decency—period. I'm for anything and everything that bodes love and consideration for my fellow man. But when lip service to some mysterious deity permits bestiality on Wednesday and absolution on Sunday—cash me out.

The big lesson in life, baby, is never be scared of anyone or anything.

Most of what has been written about me is one big blur, but I do remember being described in one simple word that I agree with. It was in a piece that tore me apart for my personal behavior, but the writer said that when the music began and I started to sing, I was *honest*.

People who make a living off other people's fortunes or misfortunes are parasites.

Rock'n'roll is a pestilential aphrodisiac, the preferred music of the delinquents.

Orange is the happiest color.

People often remark that I'm pretty lucky. Luck is only important in so far as getting the chance to sell yourself at the right moment. After that, you've got to have talent and know how to use it.

You buy a Ferrari when you want to be somebody. You buy a Lamborghini when you *are* somebody.

" I think that if you do the best you can in your life, you get your just reward. You sometimes give up a great deal to achieve a plane you're looking for.

"

A friend to me has no race, no class, and belongs to no minority.

Nothing anybody's said or written about me ever bothers me, except when it does.

You can be the most artistically perfect performer in the world, but an audience is like a broad—if you're indifferent, Endsville.

"The only male singer who I've seen besides myself and who's better than me—that is Michael Jackson.

"A friend is never an imposition."

"Nothin' but the best is good enough for me.

"

> Don't tell me. Suggest. But don't tell me.

"Never yawn in front of a lady.

"

For years I've nursed a secret desire to spend the Fourth of July in a double hammock with a swingin' redheaded broad . . . but I could never find me a double hammock.

"
What formula? I never had one, so I couldn't say what the main ingredient is. I think everybody who's successful in this business has one common ingredient—the talent God gave us. The rest depends upon how it's used.
"

> Stay alive, stay active, and get as much practice as you can.

"Make a woman feel appreciated, make her feel beautiful."

Card players have a saying: it's all right to play if you keep your eyes on the deck—which is another way of saying, eternal vigilance is the price of liberty.

Let's just say that the place isn't important, as long as everybody has a good time.

"You can't get into trouble window-shopping."

"What is the point of singing wonderful lyrics if the audience can't understand what is being said or heard?

Hello, this is a recording, you've dialed the right number, now hang up and don't do it again.

"It's not how good you do.
It's how long you do good.

You only go around once, but if you play your cards right, once is enough.

"
There are moments when it's too quiet. Particularly late at night or early in the mornings. That's when you know there's something lacking in your life. You just know.

"

Whatever else has been said about me personally is unimportant. When I sing, I believe. I'm honest.

"It is Billie Holiday who was, and still remains, the greatest single musical influence on me.

Las Vegas is the only place I know where money really talks—it says, 'Goodbye.'

"Never ignore an inner voice that tells you something could be better, even when other people tell you it's okay.

Dean Martin has been stoned more often than the United States embassies.

"
I'm trying to figure out, Chairman of what Board? People come up to me and seriously say: 'Well, what are you Chairman of?' And I can't answer them.
"

Bad reviews I've gotten never diminished the number of people in my audience; good reviews have never added to the number of people in my audience; be your own critic.

Whatever the quandary, it leaves you.

If I had done everything I'm credited with, I'd be speaking to you from a laboratory jar at Harvard Medical School.

"What I do with my life is of my own doing. I live it the best way I can.

"Don't despair. You have to scrape the bottom to appreciate life and start living again.

"

It takes a long time to heal a broken heart. It's happened to all of us and never gets any easier. I understand, however, that playing one of my albums can help.

"

As you may know, I have many good friends in the press who, unfortunately, have thus far refused to identify themselves and go public.

> Let's face it—wars you can win, Hitler you can defeat, but not a dame.

> Wake up! You know what loners are? Losers.

"Here's to absent friends—fuck 'em!"

"How's your drink? Let me taste it.

"

"I want all women to be treated like I want my wife, daughters, granddaughters to be treated.

"

I would like to be remembered as a man who had a wonderful time living life, a man who had good friends, fine family—and I don't think I could ask for anything more than that.

I think my greatest ambition in life is to pass on to others what I know.

Oh, I just wish someone would try to hurt you so I could kill them for you.

"You better get busy living, because dying's a pain in the ass.

"

It took me a long, long time to learn what I now want that to die with me.

May you live to be 100 and may the last voice you hear be mine.

Frank Sinatra

ABOUT THE EDITOR

Jade Riley is a writer whose interests include old movies, art history, vintage fashion and books, books, books.

Her dream is to move to London, to write like Virginia Woolf, and to meet a man like Mr. Darcy, who owns a vacation home in Greece.

www.ingramcontent.com/pod-product-compliance
Lightning Source LLC
Chambersburg PA
CBHW030047100526
44590CB00011B/357